CONTENTS

Chapter 1: What is EFT?	4
Chapter 2: Feelings Are Like Weather!	9
Chapter 3: Meet the Tapping Points!	15
Chapter 4: Tapping Away Worries and Fears	24
Chapter 5: Tapping Through Anger and Sadness	27
Chapter 6: Tapping for Self-Esteem and Confidence	30
Chapter 7: Tapping for School Success	34
Chapter 8: Tapping for Friendships and Social Skills	37
Chapter 9: Tapping for Healthy Habits	41
Chapter 10: Tapping for Your Dreams and Goals	45
Chapter 11: Tapping for a Kind and Caring World	49
Part V: EFT Resources and Activities	53

JACK N.RAVEN

EFT for Kids

Unlocking Emotional Freedom and Resilience in Children Through the Magic of Tapping

Jack N. Raven

No part of this book may be reproduced or transmitted in any form whatsoever, electronic, or mechanical, including photocopying, recording, or by any informational storage or retrieval system without express permission from the author.

Copyright © 2024 JNR Publishing
All rights reserved

JACK N.RAVEN

Part I: Welcome to the World of EFT!

CHAPTER 1: WHAT IS EFT?

1.1 Imagine a Magical Button Inside You!

Have you ever wished you had a magical button that could make you feel better when you're sad, scared, or angry? Imagine having a special button inside you that can turn those yucky feelings into happy ones with just a little tap! Guess what? You do have these amazing "feeling buttons" inside your body, and they can help you feel calm and joyful. This is what EFT is all about!

Let's Dive Deeper:

Think about the last time you felt really upset—maybe you lost your favorite toy or had a fight with a friend. Those feelings can be super strong, right? Now, imagine if you had a magic button that could help you calm down instantly. That's exactly what EFT offers! These "feeling buttons" are special points on your body that, when tapped gently, can help your emotions settle down.

How It Works:

EFT stands for Emotional Freedom Techniques, but you can think of it as a magical way to play with your feelings. Just like a wizard uses a magic wand to cast spells, you can use your fingers to tap on certain spots on your body to help your emotions feel better. It's like having your very own superpower to manage how you feel!

Why It's Cool:

- **Empowerment:** You get to be the hero of your own story, controlling how you feel.

- **Simplicity:** No need for complicated tools—just your fingers and a bit of focus.
- **Portability:** You can use EFT anywhere, anytime, whether you're at home, school, or even on a playground adventure!

1.2 Tapping on Your "Feeling Buttons"

Inside your body, there are lots of special "feeling buttons" connected to your emotions. When you feel scared, worried, or upset, these buttons can get stuck, kind of like when your favorite toy gets jammed and stops working right. When that happens, your feelings can feel stuck too, making you feel not so great.

Let's Explore More:

Imagine your feelings are like a river flowing through you. Sometimes, rocks and branches can block the water, causing it to pool up and create little ponds of strong emotions. Tapping on your "feeling buttons" helps remove those blocks, letting the river flow smoothly again.

Finding Your Feeling Buttons:

These magical tapping spots are located on your face, chest, and hands. Here are a few key points:

- **Karate Chop Point:** Located on the side of your hand, near your pinky finger. Imagine you're a karate master tapping this point before a big move!
- **Eyebrow Point:** Right where your eyebrow starts, near the bridge of your nose. Think of it as the starting line for your tapping adventure.
- **Side of the Eye:** On the bone at the outside corner of your eye. It's like giving yourself a little wink of calmness.
- **Under the Eye:** Just below your eye, on the cheekbone. This spot helps smooth out those emotional waves.
- **Under the Nose:** Between your nose and upper lip. A

perfect spot to clear away any lingering worries.
- **Chin Point:** Below your lower lip, right on your chin. Tap here to settle your thoughts.
- **Collarbone Point:** Just below your collarbone, where your shirt meets your neck. Imagine this as the foundation for your emotional balance.
- **Under the Arm:** On your side, about four inches below your armpit. A cool spot to anchor your feelings.
- **Top of the Head:** Right at the crown of your head. The finishing touch to your tapping routine!

Why These Points?

Each of these points is connected to different parts of your body and energy flow. By tapping on them, you send positive signals to your brain, helping to release any stuck emotions and bring back your natural sense of calm and happiness.

1.3 How EFT Helps You Feel Better

When you tap on these special points while thinking about what's bothering you, it's like sending a gentle, calming message to your brain. Imagine telling your brain, "Hey, it's okay! We've got this!" This helps your brain relax and think more clearly, making you feel better almost right away.

Understanding the Magic:

- **Focus:** By concentrating on what's bothering you while you tap, you're giving your brain clear instructions on what to address.
- **Calmness:** The tapping motion has a soothing effect, similar to how a gentle massage can help you relax.
- **Balance:** EFT helps balance your emotions, making it easier to handle tough situations without feeling overwhelmed.

Real-Life Examples:

- **Before a Big Test:** Feeling nervous? Tap on your feeling

buttons to calm your nerves and boost your confidence.
- **After a Fight:** Feeling angry or sad? Use EFT to release those strong emotions and find peace.
- **When You're Excited:** Even positive emotions can be overwhelming. Tapping helps you manage your excitement so you can enjoy it fully without feeling out of control.

Superhero Tool:

Think of EFT as your secret superhero tool that you can use anytime you need it. Whether you're facing a challenge or just want to maintain your happiness, EFT is always ready to help you feel brave, calm, and joyful. And the best part? This super tool is always with you, no matter where you go!

1.4 Let's Go on an EFT Adventure!

Are you excited to discover more about this magical tapping adventure called EFT? Get ready for a journey full of fun activities, awesome stories, and lots of tapping! You'll learn how to use EFT to feel better when you're upset, make new friends, do your best in school, and even reach for your biggest dreams.

What to Expect on This Adventure:

- **Fun Activities:** Engaging exercises that help you practice tapping and understand your emotions better.
- **Awesome Stories:** Relatable tales of kids like you who use EFT to overcome challenges and achieve their goals.
- **Interactive Lessons:** Step-by-step guides that make learning EFT easy and enjoyable.

Why Go on This Adventure?

- **Self-Discovery:** Learn more about your own feelings and how to handle them effectively.
- **Emotional Strength:** Build resilience by managing your emotions in a healthy way.
- **Positive Relationships:** Use EFT to improve how you

interact with friends and family.
- **Achieving Goals:** Whether it's doing well in school, playing a sport, or pursuing a hobby, EFT can help you stay focused and motivated.

Your Role:

You're the hero of this story! With your superhero cape on, you'll explore the amazing world of EFT, discovering how to tap your way to happiness and emotional freedom. Together, we'll embark on this incredible journey, making every day brighter and every challenge easier to handle.

CHAPTER 2: FEELINGS ARE LIKE WEATHER!

2.1 Sunny Days and Stormy Days

Have you ever noticed how the weather changes every day? Some days are bright and sunny, making you feel happy and energetic. Other days might be rainy or cloudy, making everything look a bit gloomy. Our feelings are a lot like the weather too! Sometimes we feel joyful and excited, just like a sunny day. Other times, we might feel sad or angry, like a stormy day.

Exploring the Weather-Feelings Connection:

- **Sunny Feelings:** When you're happy, excited, or calm, it's like enjoying a bright, sunny day. The sun makes everything look vibrant and full of life, just like your positive emotions make your day feel wonderful.
- **Stormy Feelings:** When you're sad, angry, or scared, it's like experiencing a thunderstorm. The loud noises and strong winds can feel overwhelming, just like those intense emotions can be hard to handle.

Why It's Okay:

Just like weather changes, your feelings will come and go. Some days you'll feel like you're basking in the sunshine, and other days you might feel like you're stuck in a storm. Both are natural and part of life's beautiful variety.

Fun Activity: Weather Journal:

Create a weather journal where you draw or write about how you feel each day. Use different weather symbols like suns, clouds, rainbows, and lightning to represent your emotions. This helps you recognize and understand your feelings better.

2.2 When Feelings Get Big and Loud

Sometimes, our feelings can become really big and loud, just like a thunderstorm. Imagine feeling so scared, angry, or sad that it feels like a huge storm is raging inside you. These strong emotions can make everything around you feel overwhelming, like trying to play outside during a wild thunderstorm.

Understanding Intense Emotions:

- **Scary Storms:** Feeling terrified or anxious can feel like dark clouds and heavy rain blocking your way.
- **Angry Storms:** Anger can be like thunder and lightning, making everything feel chaotic and out of control.
- **Sad Storms:** Sadness can feel like a constant drizzle, making everything seem gray and dull.

How EFT Helps Calm the Storm:

But here's the good news: EFT can help you calm that storm! Just like an umbrella keeps you dry in the rain, tapping on your special feeling buttons can protect you from those intense emotions. By tapping, you can help your feelings settle down, making you feel calmer and more in control, even when your emotions are as loud as thunder.

Step-by-Step Calm Down Routine:

1. **Identify the Storm:** Think about what's making you feel overwhelmed.
2. **Choose a Feeling Button:** Pick one of your special tapping points.
3. **Start Tapping:** Gently tap on the chosen point while thinking about your strong emotion.
4. **Breathe Deeply:** Take slow, deep breaths to help relax your body.

5. **Repeat as Needed:** Continue tapping until the storm starts to calm.

Example Scenario:

Imagine you're about to perform in a school play and you're feeling extremely nervous. By using EFT, you can tap on your feeling buttons to reduce your anxiety, helping you feel more confident and ready to shine on stage.

2.3 It's Okay to Feel Your Feelings

It's important to remember that all feelings are okay, even the ones that might feel uncomfortable. You might not like feeling sad or angry, but these emotions are a normal part of being human. Just like plants need rain to grow strong and healthy, we need to experience all kinds of emotions to grow and learn.

Embracing All Emotions:

- **Happy and Excited:** Feelings that make you want to jump for joy and share your happiness with others.
- **Sad and Angry:** Feelings that might make you want to cry or shout, but they help you understand what's important to you.
- **Scared and Worried:** Feelings that alert you to things that need attention or protection.

Why Every Emotion Matters:

Each emotion teaches you something about yourself and the world around you. They help you navigate through different situations, build empathy, and develop resilience.

Fun Activity: Emotion Charades:

Play a game of charades where you act out different emotions. This helps you recognize and express your feelings in a fun and interactive way.

Using EFT with All Emotions:

When you feel a strong emotion, instead of trying to ignore or push it away, use EFT to understand and manage it. This way, you're not letting the emotion take over, but instead, you're learning how to handle it in a healthy way.

2.4 EFT Can Help You Weather the Storm

No matter what kind of emotional weather you're experiencing, EFT is here to help you get through it. Whether you're basking in sunny happiness or caught in a stormy anger, tapping can be your secret tool for handling all kinds of feelings. It's like having a personal weather forecast that helps you prepare for and manage your emotions.

EFT as Your Emotional Umbrella:

Just like you wouldn't leave home without an umbrella on a rainy day, EFT is a tool you can always have ready for when your emotions get tough. It helps you stay prepared and maintain your emotional balance no matter what comes your way.

Building Your Emotional Toolkit:

- **Identify Your Emotions:** Recognize what you're feeling and label it.
- **Use EFT Tapping:** Apply the tapping technique to manage and balance your emotions.
- **Reflect and Learn:** Think about what triggered the emotion and how EFT helped, so you can use it again in the future.

Real-Life Applications:

- **School Challenges:** Feeling stressed about homework or tests? Use EFT to stay focused and calm.
- **Friendship Issues:** If you're having a disagreement with a friend, EFT can help you manage your feelings and communicate better.
- **Personal Goals:** Whether you want to learn a new skill

or achieve something important, EFT can keep you motivated and positive.

Expanding on EFT for Children

By exploring EFT through these fun and relatable ideas, children can better understand how to manage their emotions and feel empowered to take control of their feelings. Whether it's tapping through a tough day or celebrating a happy moment, EFT offers a magical way to navigate the wonderful world of emotions.

Additional Tips for Kids:

- **Consistency is Key:** Practice tapping regularly, even when you're feeling good, to make it a natural part of your routine.
- **Create a Tapping Song:** Make up a fun song that reminds you to tap your feeling buttons when you need to.
- **Share with Friends:** Teach your friends about EFT so you can all support each other in managing your emotions.
- **Use Visualization:** Imagine a peaceful place while you tap to enhance the calming effect.

Encouraging Emotional Intelligence:

EFT not only helps with immediate emotional relief but also builds emotional intelligence. Kids learn to recognize their emotions, understand their triggers, and develop healthy coping mechanisms. This foundation supports better relationships, academic success, and overall well-being.

Remember, you have the power to control your feelings and make every day a positive adventure. With EFT as your guide, you can navigate through any emotional weather, turning challenges into opportunities for growth and happiness. So, embrace your magical feeling buttons, and let's continue this exciting journey together!

Part II: Learn to Tap Your Way to Happiness!

CHAPTER 3: MEET THE TAPPING POINTS!

3.1 The "Feeling Buttons" on Your Body

Remember those special "feeling buttons" we talked about earlier? It's time to learn where they are on your body! These points are like little energy stations that can help you feel better when you tap on them. Think of them as magic spots that, when tapped, can send soothing signals to your brain to help calm your feelings.

Let's Explore the Feeling Buttons:

There are eight main tapping points that we use in EFT. Each one has its own unique spot on your body and a special name. They might sound a little funny at first, but they're super powerful tools to help you manage your emotions. Let's meet each one!

1. **The Karate Chop Point (Side of the Hand):**
    - **Location:** On the side of your hand, near your pinky finger. Imagine where you might do a karate chop!
    - **Why It's Special:** This is where you start your tapping journey. It's like giving your hand a little high-five to begin the process.
2. **The Eyebrow Point:**
    - **Location:** At the beginning of your eyebrow, closest to your nose.
    - **Why It's Special:** Tapping here helps clear your mind, just like starting a story from the beginning.

3. **The Side of the Eye Point:**
   - **Location:** On the bone at the outside corner of your eye.
   - **Why It's Special:** This spot helps you release any tension you might be feeling around your eyes.
4. **The Under the Eye Point:**
   - **Location:** On the bone under your eye, about an inch below your pupil.
   - **Why It's Special:** Tapping here helps smooth out those emotional waves, making you feel calmer.
5. **The Under the Nose Point:**
   - **Location:** Right under your nose, above your upper lip.
   - **Why It's Special:** This point helps clear away any lingering worries or stress.
6. **The Chin Point:**
   - **Location:** Right below your lower lip, in the crease of your chin.
   - **Why It's Special:** Tapping here helps settle your thoughts and bring peace to your mind.
7. **The Collarbone Point:**
   - **Location:** Just below your collarbone, where your shirt meets your neck.
   - **Why It's Special:** This is like the foundation of your emotional balance, keeping everything steady.
8. **The Under the Arm Point:**
   - **Location:** About four inches below your armpit, on the side of your body.
   - **Why It's Special:** This spot anchors your feelings, helping you stay grounded and secure.
9. **The Top of the Head Point:**
   - **Location:** Right at the crown of your head.

- **Why It's Special:** This is the finishing touch to your tapping routine, bringing everything together.

Why These Points?

Each of these points is connected to different parts of your body and energy flow. By tapping on them, you send positive signals to your brain, helping to release any stuck emotions and bring back your natural sense of calm and happiness.

3.2 Tapping with Your Fingers

Now that you know where the feeling buttons are, let's learn how to tap on them! Tapping is simple and fun, and you can do it anywhere—at home, school, or even on the playground.

How to Tap:

1. **Choose Your Finger:**
   - You can use your index finger and middle finger together, or just one finger if that feels better. It's all about what feels comfortable for you.
2. **Gently Tap:**
   - Tap gently on each point, about 5-7 times. It should never hurt—just a soft, gentle tapping, kind of like how you might tap your fingers on a table when you're thinking.
3. **Adjust if Needed:**
   - If tapping feels uncomfortable, you can always adjust the pressure or ask a grown-up for help. It's important to feel relaxed while you tap.

Let's Practice Together:

- **Start with the Karate Chop Point:** Use two fingers to tap gently.
- **Move to the Eyebrow Point:** Tap softly while saying something like, "I'm feeling [your feeling]."

- **Continue Through All Points:** Move through each tapping point, maintaining a gentle touch.

Why Use Your Fingers?

Your fingers are perfect for tapping because they're sensitive and can easily reach all the special points on your body. Plus, using your fingers helps you focus on the tapping and the feeling you want to change.

3.3 Say "Hello" to Each Tapping Point

Let's take a moment to greet each tapping point and learn exactly where they are on your body. This makes tapping more fun and helps you remember where to tap!

1. The Karate Chop Point:

- **Location:** On the side of your hand, near your pinky finger.
- **Greeting:** Say, "Hello, Karate Chop Point!" and give it a gentle tap.

2. The Eyebrow Point:

- **Location:** At the beginning of your eyebrow, closest to your nose.
- **Greeting:** Say, "Hi, Eyebrow Point!" and tap it softly.

3. The Side of the Eye Point:

- **Location:** On the bone at the outside corner of your eye.
- **Greeting:** Say, "Nice to meet you, Side of the Eye Point!" and tap gently.

4. The Under the Eye Point:

- **Location:** On the bone under your eye, about an inch below your pupil.
- **Greeting:** Say, "How's it going, Under the Eye Point?" and give it a tap.

5. The Under the Nose Point:

- **Location:** Right under your nose, above your upper lip.
- **Greeting:** Say, "What's up, Under the Nose Point?" and tap gently.

6. The Chin Point:

- **Location:** Right below your lower lip, in the crease of your chin.
- **Greeting:** Say, "Howdy, Chin Point!" and tap softly.

7. The Collarbone Point:

- **Location:** Just below your collarbone, where your shirt meets your neck.
- **Greeting:** Say, "Nice to see you, Collarbone Point!" and tap gently.

8. The Under the Arm Point:

- **Location:** About four inches below your armpit, on the side of your body.
- **Greeting:** Say, "Hello there, Under the Arm Point!" and give it a tap.

9. The Top of the Head Point:

- **Location:** Right at the crown of your head.
- **Greeting:** Say, "Hi, Top of the Head Point!" and tap softly.

Why Greet Each Point?

Greeting each tapping point makes the process more engaging and helps you connect with each spot. It turns tapping into a friendly interaction, making it easier to remember and use whenever you need it.

3.4 Let's Practice Tapping Together!

Now that you know where all the tapping points are and how to tap on them, it's time to practice! Let's go through a simple tapping sequence together. Follow along and feel the magic of EFT.

Simple Tapping Sequence:

1. **Start with the Karate Chop Point:**
    - **Tap:** Use two fingers to tap on the Karate Chop Point.
    - **Say:** "Even though I feel [name the feeling], I'm okay. I'm a good kid."
2. **Move to the Eyebrow Point:**
    - **Tap:** Gently tap on the Eyebrow Point.
    - **Say:** "This [feeling]."
3. **Side of the Eye Point:**
    - **Tap:** Tap on the Side of the Eye Point.
    - **Say:** "I feel it in my body."
4. **Under the Eye Point:**
    - **Tap:** Tap on the Under the Eye Point.
    - **Say:** "It's okay to feel this way."
5. **Under the Nose Point:**
    - **Tap:** Tap on the Under the Nose Point.
    - **Say:** "I'm safe."
6. **Chin Point:**
    - **Tap:** Tap on the Chin Point.
    - **Say:** "I can handle this."
7. **Collarbone Point:**
    - **Tap:** Tap on the Collarbone Point.
    - **Say:** "I'm strong and brave."
8. **Under the Arm Point:**
    - **Tap:** Tap on the Under the Arm Point.
    - **Say:** "I choose to feel calm and happy."
9. **Top of the Head Point:**
    - **Tap:** Tap on the Top of the Head Point.
    - **Say:** "I am calm and happy."
10. **Take a Deep Breath:**
    - **Breathe:** Take a slow, deep breath in and out.
    - **Notice:** Pay attention to how you feel now. Do you feel a little better?

Repeat if Needed:

If you still feel the uncomfortable feeling, you can repeat the tapping sequence again. Sometimes it takes a few rounds to fully feel better, and that's perfectly okay!

Why Practice Tapping?

- **Builds Confidence:** The more you practice, the more confident you become in using EFT.
- **Feels Natural:** Tapping becomes a natural response when you're feeling strong emotions.
- **Empowers You:** You learn that you have the power to change how you feel, anytime you need to.

Fun Practice Activity:

- **Tapping Buddy:** Pair up with a friend or family member and practice tapping together. You can take turns tapping on each other's shoulders to make it fun!
- **Tapping Storytime:** Create a short story where the main character uses EFT to overcome a challenge. Share your story with friends or family.

Looking Ahead:

Remember, practice makes perfect! The more you tap, the easier and more natural it will feel. In the next chapters, you'll learn how to use these tapping points to help with specific feelings and situations, like dealing with worries, calming anger, and bringing more joy into your life.

Expanding on Chapter 3 for Kids

By learning about the tapping points and practicing tapping, you're gaining a valuable tool to help manage your emotions. Here are some extra tips and fun ideas to make tapping even more enjoyable and effective:

Additional Tips for Kids:

- **Create a Tapping Chart:** Draw or print out a chart with all the tapping points and hang it somewhere you can see it, like your bedroom or play area. This helps you remember where each point is.
- **Use a Timer:** Set a timer for 5 minutes and practice tapping whenever you need a quick emotional boost.
- **Personalize Your Phrases:** Make up your own phrases that resonate with you. Instead of "I'm a good kid," you could say, "I'm doing my best."

Fun Ideas to Enhance Your Tapping Practice:

- **Tapping Songs:** Create a catchy song that includes the names of the tapping points and the tapping sequence. Singing while tapping can make the process more fun and memorable.
- **Tapping Art:** Draw pictures of each tapping point and decorate them with colors and designs that make you feel happy and relaxed.
- **Tapping Games:** Turn tapping into a game by timing yourself to see how quickly you can tap through all the points while maintaining a steady rhythm.

Encouraging Emotional Intelligence:

EFT not only helps with immediate emotional relief but also builds emotional intelligence. Here's how:

- **Recognize Emotions:** By tapping, you become more aware of what you're feeling and why.
- **Understand Triggers:** You learn to identify what causes certain emotions, helping you anticipate and manage them better.
- **Healthy Coping Mechanisms:** EFT provides a healthy way to handle emotions, reducing the need for less effective or harmful coping strategies.

Final Thought:

You're doing an amazing job learning about EFT and how to use the tapping points to manage your emotions. Remember, you have the power to control your feelings and make every day a positive adventure. With practice, tapping will become a natural and effective tool in your emotional toolkit, helping you navigate through any challenge with confidence and calmness.

So, keep practicing, stay curious, and enjoy the wonderful journey of mastering EFT. You're on your way to becoming an EFT expert, ready to handle whatever emotions come your way with ease and grace!

By exploring the tapping points through these detailed and engaging explanations, children can better understand how EFT works and feel empowered to use it whenever they need to manage their emotions. Whether it's a tough day at school or a big event, EFT offers a magical way to navigate the wonderful world of feelings.

CHAPTER 4: TAPPING AWAY WORRIES AND FEARS

4.1 When Worries Creep into Your Mind

Worries and fears can feel like pesky little creatures that creep into your mind and make you feel uneasy. Maybe you're worried about a test at school, a monster under your bed, or something bad happening to your loved ones.

When these worries show up, they can make your tummy feel tight, your heart race, or your hands get sweaty. That's your body's way of telling you that you're feeling anxious or scared.

But here's the good news: You have a secret weapon to help you chase those worries away - EFT!

4.2 Tapping for Fears Big and Small

No matter how big or small your fear is, tapping can help. Here's how you can use EFT to feel braver and more at ease:

1. First, think about what's worrying you. It might be a specific situation, like giving a presentation in class, or a general feeling, like being afraid of the dark.
2. Give your fear a number on a scale of 0-10, with 0 being not scared at all and 10 being the most scared you can imagine. This helps you see how much the fear is affecting you.
3. Now, start tapping! Begin at the Karate Chop Point and

say, "Even though I'm scared of [name the fear], I'm a brave kid. I can handle this."
 4. Then, tap through the other points, using reminder phrases like:
     - Eyebrow Point: This fear
     - Side of the Eye Point: I feel it in my body
     - Under the Eye Point: It's okay to feel scared
     - Under the Nose Point: I'm safe right now
     - Chin Point: I can be brave
     - Collarbone Point: I trust myself
     - Under the Arm Point: I choose to feel calm and confident
 5. Take a deep breath and check in with your fear level again. Has the number gone down? If it's still high, you can repeat the tapping sequence until it feels lower.

Remember, it's okay if the fear doesn't go away completely. EFT is a tool to help you manage your worries, not make them disappear forever. With practice, you'll get better and better at tapping through your fears.

4.3 Magic Words to Help You Feel Brave

In addition to tapping, you can use special "magic words" to help you feel braver and more confident. These are positive phrases that you say to yourself while tapping, like:

- "I am safe and loved."
- "I can handle whatever comes my way."
- "I trust my ability to get through this."
- "I am stronger than my fears."
- "I choose to focus on the good."

Try making up your own magic words that feel powerful and comforting to you. You can even make them silly, like "I am a brave banana!" or "Worries, schmurries, I've got this!" The more you use these phrases while tapping, the more you'll start to believe them.

4.4 Tapping Together for a Worry-Free Day

Let's put all of this together and do a tapping sequence for a worry-free day:

1. Karate Chop Point: "Even though I sometimes worry about things, I'm a capable kid. I can handle my worries one tap at a time."
2. Eyebrow Point: These worries
3. Side of the Eye Point: They feel big sometimes
4. Under the Eye Point: But I'm bigger than my worries
5. Under the Nose Point: I can tap them away
6. Chin Point: And feel more peaceful inside
7. Collarbone Point: I trust myself to handle what comes
8. Under the Arm Point: I choose to have a worry-free day

Take a deep breath and imagine yourself having a day where worries don't get in the way. You are brave, you are strong, and with EFT, you can face your fears with confidence!

CHAPTER 5: TAPPING THROUGH ANGER AND SADNESS

5.1 When Anger Makes You Hot

Anger is a fiery feeling that can make you feel hot all over. Maybe your little brother broke your favorite toy, or a friend said something mean to you at school. When you're angry, you might feel like yelling, hitting, or throwing things.

But here's the thing: while it's okay to feel angry, it's not okay to hurt yourself or others. That's where EFT comes in - it can help you cool down that hot anger and find a more peaceful way to handle the situation.

Here's how you can tap when you're feeling angry:

1. Karate Chop Point: "Even though I'm really angry right now, I'm a good kid. I can handle this anger."
2. Eyebrow Point: This hot anger
3. Side of the Eye Point: I feel it in my body
4. Under the Eye Point: It's okay to feel angry
5. Under the Nose Point: I can let this anger go
6. Chin Point: I choose to cool down
7. Collarbone Point: I can find a peaceful solution
8. Under the Arm Point: I'm in control of my feelings

Take some deep breaths and notice how your body feels. Is the anger starting to melt away? Keep tapping until you feel calmer and more in control.

5.2 When Sadness Makes You Cry

Sadness is a heavy feeling that can make you feel like crying. Maybe you miss someone who moved away, or your pet fish died. When you're sad, you might feel like staying in bed all day or hiding under the covers.

It's okay to feel sad - it's a normal part of life. But when sadness starts to take over, tapping can help you find a glimmer of hope and happiness again. Here's how you can tap when you're feeling sad:

1. Karate Chop Point: "Even though I'm feeling really sad right now, I'm a good kid. It's okay to feel this way."
2. Eyebrow Point: This heavy sadness
3. Side of the Eye Point: I feel it in my heart
4. Under the Eye Point: It's okay to cry
5. Under the Nose Point: I can let this sadness out
6. Chin Point: I won't feel this way forever
7. Collarbone Point: I'm loved and supported
8. Under the Arm Point: I choose to find a little happiness today

Keep tapping and take some slow, deep breaths. Imagine the sadness starting to lift, like a heavy blanket being pulled off of you. You are strong, you are resilient, and you can get through this tough feeling.

5.3 Tapping for a Calm and Peaceful Heart

When you're feeling angry or sad, your heart might feel like it's in a stormy, chaotic place. Tapping can help bring a sense of calm and peace to your heart, like a soothing balm.

Try this tapping sequence for a calm and peaceful heart:

1. Karate Chop Point: "Even though my heart feels stormy right now, I'm okay. I can find peace."
2. Eyebrow Point: This chaos in my heart

are. Being kind to yourself is a gift that you deserve.

6.2 Finding Your Inner Strengths

Everyone has inner strengths and talents, even if they're not always easy to see. Maybe you're really good at making people laugh, or you're a great listener when a friend is upset. Maybe you're creative, brave, or kind.

Take a moment to think about your own inner strengths. What are you proud of about yourself? What do you like about who you are?

Now, let's tap on those strengths:

1. Karate Chop Point: "Even though I sometimes forget my strengths, I have so many amazing qualities. I choose to recognize and celebrate them."
2. Eyebrow Point: My inner strengths
3. Side of the Eye Point: I have so many talents
4. Under the Eye Point: I'm proud of who I am
5. Under the Nose Point: I choose to focus on my positives
6. Chin Point: I'm a uniquely amazing person
7. Collarbone Point: My strengths make me shine
8. Under the Arm Point: I love and appreciate myself

The more you focus on your strengths and the things you like about yourself, the more those qualities will grow. You'll start to feel more confident and secure in who you are.

6.3 Tapping for a Powerful "I Can!" Feeling

When you believe in yourself and your abilities, you feel like you can take on the world! This is the "I Can!" feeling - a sense of empowerment and confidence that comes from within.

Sometimes, when we're facing a challenge or trying something new, we might feel unsure or doubtful. That's when we need to tap into our "I Can!" power. Here's how:

1. Karate Chop Point: "Even though I feel unsure about

this, I choose to believe in myself. I have what it takes to succeed."
2. Eyebrow Point: This doubt I'm feeling
3. Side of the Eye Point: I'm not sure if I can do it
4. Under the Eye Point: But I'm braver than I think
5. Under the Nose Point: I have the strength inside me
6. Chin Point: I choose to believe in myself
7. Collarbone Point: I tap into my "I Can!" power
8. Under the Arm Point: I can do amazing things!

Every time you face a new challenge, remind yourself: "I Can!" You are capable, strong, and ready to take on whatever comes your way.

6.4 Believing in Yourself, One Tap at a Time

Building self-esteem and confidence is a journey, and EFT can be your companion along the way. Each time you tap, you're sending a loving, supportive message to yourself. You're saying, "I believe in you, I support you, and I know you can handle anything."

Here's a final tapping sequence to boost your self-belief:

1. Karate Chop Point: "Even though I'm still learning to believe in myself, I choose to take it one step at a time. I'm making progress every day."
2. Eyebrow Point: I'm learning to believe in me
3. Side of the Eye Point: One tap at a time
4. Under the Eye Point: I'm growing in confidence
5. Under the Nose Point: I trust in my abilities
6. Chin Point: I can achieve great things
7. Collarbone Point: I'm proud of my journey
8. Under the Arm Point: I choose to believe in the amazing me!

Remember, you are a work in progress, and that's a beautiful thing. Keep tapping, keep believing in yourself, and watch your self-esteem and confidence soar!

Part III: EFT for Everyday Adventures

CHAPTER 7: TAPPING FOR SCHOOL SUCCESS

7.1 Tapping for a Calm and Focused Mind

School can be exciting and fun, but it can also feel stressful sometimes. Maybe you're worried about a big test, or you're having trouble focusing on your homework. When your mind feels jumbled and anxious, it's hard to do your best in school.

EFT can help you calm your mind and find your focus. Try this tapping sequence before a test or when you're studying:

1. Karate Chop Point: "Even though I feel stressed about school, I choose to relax and focus. I can do this."
2. Eyebrow Point: This school stress
3. Side of the Eye Point: My mind feels jumbled
4. Under the Eye Point: It's hard to focus
5. Under the Nose Point: But I can find my calm
6. Chin Point: I breathe in peace and clarity
7. Collarbone Point: I choose to focus on what I know
8. Under the Arm Point: I trust my mind to guide me

Take a few deep breaths and feel your mind settling. You are capable of learning and understanding. You have what it takes to succeed in school.

7.2 Tapping Away Test Anxiety

Tests and exams can be scary, even when you've studied hard. You might worry about forgetting everything you learned, or not being good enough. This is called test anxiety, and it's a very common feeling.

Here's how you can tap through test anxiety:

1. Karate Chop Point: "Even though I'm worried about this test, I choose to trust in what I've learned. I can handle this."
2. Eyebrow Point: This test anxiety
3. Side of the Eye Point: I'm afraid I'll forget everything
4. Under the Eye Point: Or that I'm not good enough
5. Under the Nose Point: But I've prepared for this
6. Chin Point: I choose to trust in my knowledge
7. Collarbone Point: I release this anxious feeling
8. Under the Arm Point: I am calm, confident, and ready

Remember, a test is just a way to show what you know. It doesn't define your worth or intelligence. You are so much more than a test score!

7.3 Tapping for Better Concentration

Sometimes, it can be hard to concentrate in school, especially if the subject is challenging or the classroom is noisy. When you're having trouble focusing, EFT can help you find your center and engage your mind.

Try this tapping sequence to boost your concentration:

1. Karate Chop Point: "Even though I'm having trouble focusing, I choose to be present and engaged. I can concentrate."
2. Eyebrow Point: This distracted feeling
3. Side of the Eye Point: It's hard to pay attention
4. Under the Eye Point: My mind wants to wander
5. Under the Nose Point: But I choose to be present
6. Chin Point: I focus on what's in front of me
7. Collarbone Point: I engage my mind and my senses
8. Under the Arm Point: I am focused, attentive, and learning

Take a moment to tune into your surroundings. What can you see, hear, feel, and learn in this moment? The more present you are, the easier it is to concentrate.

7.4 Tapping for a Love of Learning

Learning is an adventure, and school is full of opportunities to discover new things. When you approach school with curiosity and excitement, everything becomes more fun and interesting.

Here's a tapping sequence to help you find your love of learning:

1. Karate Chop Point: "Even though school can be challenging sometimes, I choose to approach it with curiosity and joy. I love to learn."
2. Eyebrow Point: School is an adventure
3. Side of the Eye Point: So much to discover
4. Under the Eye Point: I open my mind to new ideas
5. Under the Nose Point: I find joy in learning
6. Chin Point: Every day is a chance to grow
7. Collarbone Point: I am curious and excited
8. Under the Arm Point: I love exploring the world through learning

Remember, you are a natural-born learner. Your mind is amazing, and it's capable of understanding so many wonderful things. Approach school with a sense of wonder, and watch your love of learning grow!

CHAPTER 8: TAPPING FOR FRIENDSHIPS AND SOCIAL SKILLS

8.1 Tapping for Making New Friends

Making new friends can be scary, especially if you're shy or feeling unsure of yourself. You might worry about what to say, or whether people will like you. These are normal feelings, and EFT can help you feel more confident and open to new friendships.

Try this tapping sequence before a social situation where you want to make new friends:

1. Karate Chop Point: "Even though I'm nervous about making new friends, I choose to be open and confident. I am worthy of friendship."
2. Eyebrow Point: This nervousness about new friends
3. Side of the Eye Point: I'm not sure what to say
4. Under the Eye Point: Or if they'll like me
5. Under the Nose Point: But I am a good friend
6. Chin Point: I have so much to offer
7. Collarbone Point: I choose to be open and friendly
8. Under the Arm Point: I attract wonderful friends into my life

Remember, everyone feels nervous about making new friends sometimes. The key is to be yourself, show interest in others, and let your unique light shine. You have so much to offer in a friendship!

8.2 Tapping for Dealing with Conflicts

Even the best of friends can have conflicts and disagreements sometimes. Maybe your friend said something hurtful, or you're having trouble sharing and taking turns. When conflicts happen, it's important to find a way to communicate and resolve the issue.

Here's how you can tap when you're dealing with a conflict with a friend:

1. Karate Chop Point: "Even though I'm upset with my friend, I choose to find a peaceful solution. Our friendship is worth working through this."
2. Eyebrow Point: This conflict with my friend
3. Side of the Eye Point: I'm feeling hurt and angry
4. Under the Eye Point: It's hard to see their side
5. Under the Nose Point: But I value our friendship
6. Chin Point: I choose to communicate openly
7. Collarbone Point: I'm open to finding a solution
8. Under the Arm Point: We can work through this together

After tapping, take a deep breath and approach your friend with a calm and open heart. Listen to their side, express your feelings, and work together to find a solution that feels good for both of you. Remember, conflicts are opportunities to strengthen your friendship and learn more about each other.

8.3 Tapping for Kindness and Compassion

One of the most important qualities in a friend is kindness and compassion. When you approach others with an open heart and a desire to understand, your friendships will be filled with love and support.

Here's a tapping sequence to help you cultivate kindness and compassion:

1. Karate Chop Point: "Even though it's not always easy, I choose to approach others with kindness and

compassion. I open my heart to understanding."
2. Eyebrow Point: Sometimes it's hard to be kind
3. Side of the Eye Point: Especially when I'm feeling hurt
4. Under the Eye Point: But I choose to see the best in others
5. Under the Nose Point: I tap into my compassion
6. Chin Point: I seek to understand, not judge
7. Collarbone Point: Kindness is my superpower
8. Under the Arm Point: I spread love and compassion wherever I go

Remember, everyone is fighting a battle you know nothing about. When you choose to be kind, even in difficult situations, you make the world a little bit brighter for everyone.

8.4 Tapping for Happy and Healthy Relationships

Friendships are one of the greatest joys in life. They bring laughter, support, and love into your world. When you nurture your friendships with care and attention, they grow stronger and deeper over time.

Here's a final tapping sequence to help you create happy and healthy friendships:

1. Karate Chop Point: "Even though friendships can be challenging sometimes, I choose to nurture them with love and care. I am grateful for the friends in my life."
2. Eyebrow Point: I'm learning and growing in my friendships
3. Side of the Eye Point: I choose to be a good friend
4. Under the Eye Point: I communicate openly and honestly
5. Under the Nose Point: I appreciate my friends' unique qualities
6. Chin Point: I surround myself with positive, supportive people
7. Collarbone Point: My friendships are a source of joy and

love
8. Under the Arm Point: I am grateful for the gift of friendship

Take a moment to think about your friends and all the wonderful moments you've shared together. Send them a silent "thank you" for being in your life. With each tap, feel your heart filling with love and appreciation for the magic of friendship.

CHAPTER 9: TAPPING FOR HEALTHY HABITS

9.1 Tapping for a Good Night's Sleep

Sleep is like a superpower that helps you feel your best. When you get enough rest, you have more energy, focus, and happiness throughout the day. But sometimes, it can be hard to fall asleep or stay asleep through the night.

EFT can help you relax your body and mind for a peaceful, restful sleep. Try this tapping sequence before bedtime:

1. Karate Chop Point: "Even though I sometimes have trouble sleeping, I choose to relax and allow myself to rest. My body knows how to find peaceful sleep."
2. Eyebrow Point: This trouble falling asleep
3. Side of the Eye Point: My mind is racing with thoughts
4. Under the Eye Point: My body feels restless
5. Under the Nose Point: But I choose to let go and relax
6. Chin Point: I release the day's worries and stresses
7. Collarbone Point: I allow myself to sink into peace
8. Under the Arm Point: I am ready for a restful, rejuvenating sleep

After tapping, take a few deep breaths and imagine yourself drifting off into a peaceful, dreamland sleep. Trust that your body knows how to rest and recharge. Sweet dreams!

9.2 Tapping for Healthy Eating

Eating healthy foods is like giving your body a big hug. When you nourish yourself with fruits, veggies, and wholesome meals, you feel energized, strong, and vibrant. But sometimes, it can be tempting to reach for sugary or processed snacks instead.

Here's how you can tap for healthy eating choices:

1. Karate Chop Point: "Even though I'm tempted by unhealthy snacks, I choose to nourish my body with wholesome foods. I love feeling healthy and strong."
2. Eyebrow Point: This craving for sugary snacks
3. Side of the Eye Point: It's hard to resist sometimes
4. Under the Eye Point: But I know how good healthy food makes me feel
5. Under the Nose Point: I choose to listen to my body's wisdom
6. Chin Point: I nourish myself with rainbow fruits and veggies
7. Collarbone Point: Healthy eating is an act of self-love
8. Under the Arm Point: I am proud of my healthy choices

Remember, it's okay to enjoy treats sometimes. The key is to find a balance and to choose foods that make you feel good inside and out. Listen to your body, and trust that it knows what it needs to thrive.

9.3 Tapping for Staying Active and Strong

Moving your body is like giving it a big "thank you" for all it does for you. When you run, jump, dance, and play, you're celebrating your amazing, strong, capable body. Exercise can also help you feel happier, calmer, and more focused.

But sometimes, it can be hard to find the motivation to get moving. That's where EFT comes in - it can help you tap into your natural love of movement and activity.

Here's a tapping sequence for staying active and strong:

1. Karate Chop Point: "Even though I don't always feel like exercising, I choose to honor my body with joyful

movement. I love feeling active and strong."
2. Eyebrow Point: This resistance to exercise
3. Side of the Eye Point: I don't feel motivated sometimes
4. Under the Eye Point: But I know how good it feels to move
5. Under the Nose Point: I choose to find activities I enjoy
6. Chin Point: Dancing, playing, running free
7. Collarbone Point: I celebrate my body with movement
8. Under the Arm Point: I am active, strong, and thriving

Remember, exercise doesn't have to be a chore. Find activities that bring you joy, whether it's dancing in your room, playing tag with friends, or going on a nature hike with your family. When you approach movement with a sense of fun and celebration, staying active becomes a natural part of your life.

9.4 Tapping for a Happy and Healthy Life

Taking care of your body, mind, and heart is the key to living a happy and healthy life. When you make self-care a priority, you're filling your own cup so that you can show up fully for yourself and others.

Here's a final tapping sequence to help you embrace a healthy, joyful lifestyle:

1. Karate Chop Point: "Even though taking care of myself can feel challenging sometimes, I choose to make my health and happiness a priority. I am worth the effort."
2. Eyebrow Point: I'm learning to take care of myself
3. Side of the Eye Point: One healthy choice at a time
4. Under the Eye Point: I listen to my body's needs
5. Under the Nose Point: I nourish myself with wholesome foods
6. Chin Point: I move my body in joyful ways
7. Collarbone Point: I make time for rest and relaxation
8. Under the Arm Point: I am creating a happy, healthy life

Remember, taking care of yourself is not selfish - it's necessary.

When you prioritize your own well-being, you have more energy, love, and positivity to share with the world. You deserve to feel your best, inside and out. Keep tapping, keep making healthy choices, and watch your happiness and vitality soar!

Part IV: EFT for a Brighter Future

CHAPTER 10: TAPPING FOR YOUR DREAMS AND GOALS

10.1 What Do You Want to Be When You Grow Up?

Have you ever thought about what you want to be when you grow up? Maybe you want to be a doctor, an artist, a teacher, or an astronaut. Maybe you have a big dream that feels exciting and a little bit scary.

Whatever your dream is, it's important to remember that you have the power to make it happen. Your future is like a big, bright canvas, and you get to choose what colors and shapes to paint on it.

Take a moment to close your eyes and imagine yourself in the future, living your dream life. What do you see? How do you feel? Let that vision fill you up with excitement and joy.

Now, let's tap on that dream:

1. Karate Chop Point: "Even though my dream feels big and far away sometimes, I choose to believe in myself and my ability to make it happen. I am the creator of my future."
2. Eyebrow Point: This big, bright dream of mine
3. Side of the Eye Point: It feels so exciting and a little scary
4. Under the Eye Point: But I know I have what it takes
5. Under the Nose Point: I am capable of amazing things

6. Chin Point: I choose to believe in myself and my dreams
7. Collarbone Point: I take steps towards my future every day
8. Under the Arm Point: I am creating a life I love!

Remember, your dreams are valid and valuable, no matter how big or small they may seem. You have unique talents and gifts to offer the world, and your future is waiting for you to shape it. Keep dreaming big and believing in yourself!

10.2 Tapping for Courage and Determination

Going after your dreams takes courage and determination. There will be times when you face obstacles or setbacks, and you might feel like giving up. But that's when your inner strength and resilience will shine through.

Here's a tapping sequence to help you find your courage and determination:

1. Karate Chop Point: "Even though chasing my dreams can be scary and hard sometimes, I choose to be brave and keep going. I have courage and determination in my heart."
2. Eyebrow Point: This fear of going after my dreams
3. Side of the Eye Point: What if I fail or make mistakes?
4. Under the Eye Point: But mistakes are how I learn and grow
5. Under the Nose Point: I choose to be brave and take chances
6. Chin Point: I am determined to keep going, no matter what
7. Collarbone Point: I have the strength to overcome any obstacle
8. Under the Arm Point: I am courageous, resilient, and unstoppable!

Remember, courage doesn't mean you're never afraid. It means you feel the fear and take action anyway. Every time you face a challenge or step outside your comfort zone, you're growing stronger and braver. Keep tapping into your inner courage and determination, and trust that you can handle whatever comes your way.

10.3 Tapping for a Positive Mindset

Your thoughts and beliefs have a big impact on your life and your ability to achieve your dreams. When you focus on positive, empowering thoughts, you feel more confident, motivated, and capable of making your dreams a reality.

Here's a tapping sequence to help you cultivate a positive mindset:

1. Karate Chop Point: "Even though negative thoughts creep in sometimes, I choose to focus on the positive. I am in control of my mindset and my future."
2. Eyebrow Point: These negative, doubtful thoughts
3. Side of the Eye Point: They make me feel small and unsure
4. Under the Eye Point: But I choose to shift my focus
5. Under the Nose Point: I think thoughts that uplift and empower me
6. Chin Point: I believe in myself and my abilities
7. Collarbone Point: I trust in the power of positivity
8. Under the Arm Point: I am confident, capable, and creating my best life!

Remember, you are the master of your mind. You get to choose what thoughts and beliefs you focus on. When you catch yourself thinking something negative or self-doubting, acknowledge it, then consciously choose a more positive thought to replace it. With practice, positive thinking will become a natural, empowering habit.

10.4 Reach for the Stars, One Tap at a Time

Your dreams and goals are like stars in the sky - they may seem far away, but they're always there, guiding you forward. Every time you tap, you're taking a step closer to those shining stars and the amazing future that awaits you.

Here's a final tapping sequence to help you reach for your dreams, one tap at a time:

1. Karate Chop Point: "Even though the journey to my dreams can feel long and uncertain sometimes, I choose to trust the process and keep reaching for the stars. Every tap brings me closer to my amazing future."
2. Eyebrow Point: This journey to my dreams
3. Side of the Eye Point: It's not always easy or clear
4. Under the Eye Point: But I trust that I'm on the right path
5. Under the Nose Point: Every step, every tap, matters
6. Chin Point: I am making progress, even when I can't see it
7. Collarbone Point: I keep my eyes on the stars and my feet on the ground
8. Under the Arm Point: I am reaching for my dreams, one tap at a time!

Remember, the journey to your dreams is just as important as the destination. Every challenge you face, every lesson you learn, every tap you do - it's all part of your unique story and the amazing person you're becoming. Trust the journey, keep reaching for those stars, and know that your brightest future is on its way.

CHAPTER 11: TAPPING FOR A KIND AND CARING WORLD

11.1 Being Kind to Yourself and Others

One of the most powerful ways to create a better world is by being kind - both to yourself and to others. When you treat yourself with compassion and understanding, it's easier to extend that same kindness outward.

Here's a tapping sequence to help you cultivate kindness:

1. Karate Chop Point: "Even though it's not always easy, I choose to be kind to myself and others. I have the power to make the world a little bit brighter."
2. Eyebrow Point: Sometimes it's hard to be kind
3. Side of the Eye Point: Especially when I'm feeling hurt or angry
4. Under the Eye Point: But I choose to respond with compassion
5. Under the Nose Point: I treat myself with patience and understanding
6. Chin Point: I extend that same kindness to others
7. Collarbone Point: I look for ways to be helpful and caring
8. Under the Arm Point: I am a force for kindness in the world

Remember, kindness starts with you. When you're gentle and loving with yourself, it naturally overflows into your interactions with others. Look for small ways to be kind every day, whether it's giving yourself a break when you make a mistake, or offering a smile to someone who seems sad. Every act of kindness creates a ripple effect of positivity in the world.

11.2 Tapping for Empathy and Understanding

Empathy is the ability to put yourself in someone else's shoes and understand their feelings and experiences. When you approach others with empathy and a desire to understand, you build bridges of connection and compassion.

Here's a tapping sequence to help you develop empathy:

1. Karate Chop Point: "Even though it's not always easy to understand others, I choose to approach them with an open heart and mind. I seek to understand, not judge."
2. Eyebrow Point: It's hard to understand sometimes
3. Side of the Eye Point: When people think and act differently than me
4. Under the Eye Point: But I choose to be curious, not critical
5. Under the Nose Point: I put myself in their shoes
6. Chin Point: I seek to understand their perspective
7. Collarbone Point: I listen with an open heart
8. Under the Arm Point: I am growing in empathy and understanding

Remember, everyone has a unique story and set of experiences that shape who they are. When you approach others with empathy and a genuine desire to understand, you create space for authentic connection and growth. Practice listening more than you speak, and seeking to understand before being understood. The more you empathize with others, the more compassion and understanding you'll cultivate in your own heart.

11.3 Tapping for a More Peaceful World

Peace begins with you. When you choose to respond to conflicts and challenges with calmness, wisdom, and love, you contribute to a more peaceful world. EFT can help you find that inner peace and spread it outward.

Here's a tapping sequence for cultivating peace:

1. Karate Chop Point: "Even though the world can feel chaotic and divided sometimes, I choose to be a force for peace. I cultivate calmness and wisdom in my own heart."
2. Eyebrow Point: This chaos and conflict in the world
3. Side of the Eye Point: It can feel overwhelming and scary
4. Under the Eye Point: But I choose to focus on what I can control
5. Under the Nose Point: I breathe in peace and breathe out stress
6. Chin Point: I respond to challenges with wisdom and love
7. Collarbone Point: I am a calming presence for others
8. Under the Arm Point: I am contributing to a more peaceful world

Remember, you don't have to solve all the world's problems on your own. But you can make a difference by choosing peace in your own thoughts, words, and actions. When you encounter conflicts or disagreements, take a deep breath and choose to respond with calmness and understanding. As you cultivate more peace within yourself, you naturally inspire others to do the same. Together, one peaceful choice at a time, we can create a more harmonious world.

11.4 Spread Joy and Kindness with Every Tap

EFT is a powerful tool for creating positive change - not just in your own life, but in the world around you. Every time you tap, you're not only helping yourself feel better, but you're also contributing to a ripple effect of joy and kindness.

Here's a final tapping sequence to help you spread more light in the world:

1. Karate Chop Point: "Even though the world can feel dark and heavy sometimes, I choose to be a light. I spread joy and kindness with every tap."
2. Eyebrow Point: There's so much suffering in the world
3. Side of the Eye Point: It can feel like I can't make a difference
4. Under the Eye Point: But every small act of kindness matters
5. Under the Nose Point: I choose to be a force for good
6. Chin Point: I look for ways to make others smile
7. Collarbone Point: I tap for more joy, peace, and love
8. Under the Arm Point: I am making the world a little bit brighter, one tap at a time

Remember, you have a unique light to share with the world. Every time you choose kindness, empathy, and joy, you're making a positive impact on those around you. Keep tapping, keep shining your light, and trust that you're part of a big, beautiful tapestry of positive change. Together, we can create a world where every child feels loved, safe, and empowered to make their brightest dreams a reality.

PART V: EFT RESOURCES AND ACTIVITIES

Appendix A: EFT Games and Activities

Tapping can be even more fun when you make it into a game or activity! Here are some ideas to try:

1. Tapping Simon Says: Play a game of "Simon Says" with tapping points. Take turns being the leader and calling out tapping points for everyone to tap on. For example, "Simon says tap on your eyebrow point!"
2. Tapping Charades: Write down different emotions or situations on slips of paper and put them in a hat. Take turns drawing a slip and acting out the emotion or situation while others guess what it is. Once they guess correctly, everyone taps on that feeling together.
3. Tapping Art: Draw a picture of how you're feeling before tapping. Then, do a round of tapping on that feeling. After tapping, draw a new picture of how you feel now. Notice how your art changes after tapping!
4. Tapping Stories: Make up a story together, and every time a character in the story feels a strong emotion, pause and do a round of tapping on that feeling. See how the story changes and evolves as the characters tap through their challenges.
5. Tapping Scavenger Hunt: Go on a scavenger hunt to

find things that evoke different emotions - something that makes you happy, something that makes you feel peaceful, something that makes you feel excited, etc. Every time you find an item, do a round of tapping on that feeling.

Remember, the more fun and playful you make tapping, the more you'll want to do it! Get creative and come up with your own tapping games and activities. The possibilities are endless!

Appendix B: EFT for Parents and Caregivers

As a parent or caregiver, you play a vital role in supporting your child's emotional well-being. Here are some tips for incorporating EFT into your family life:

1. Tap along with your child: When your child is feeling a strong emotion, offer to tap along with them. This shows them that their feelings are valid and that you're there to support them through the tough stuff.
2. Make tapping a daily habit: Set aside a few minutes each day to tap as a family. You can tap on the day's events, any challenges or victories you experienced, or simply tap for a calm and peaceful day ahead.
3. Model tapping for your own emotions: Children learn by watching the adults in their lives. When you're feeling stressed, anxious, or overwhelmed, let your child see you tapping through those feelings. This normalizes the process of managing emotions in a healthy way.
4. Create a tapping corner: Designate a special space in your home for tapping, with comfy pillows, calming decorations, and tapping reminder charts. Encourage your child to visit the tapping corner whenever they need a little emotional support.
5. Praise your child's tapping efforts: When you see your child using tapping to manage their emotions, celebrate their efforts! Remind them how proud you are of them

for taking care of their emotional health. Remember, your child looks to you for guidance and support as they navigate the ups and downs of growing up. By making EFT a regular part of your family life, you're giving your child a powerful tool for emotional resilience and well-being that will serve them for years to come.

Appendix C: Recommended EFT Resources

Want to learn more about EFT and how to use it with your child? Check out these recommended resources:

1. The Tapping Solution Foundation - This non-profit organization offers a variety of free EFT resources, including tapping scripts, videos, and articles specifically for children and families. Visit their website at www.tappingsolutionfoundation.org.
2. "The Wizard's Wish: Or How He Made the Yuckies Go Away - A Story About the Magic in You" by Brad Yates - This delightful children's book tells the story of a young boy who learns to tap away his "yuckies" with the help of a wise wizard. A great introduction to EFT for kids!
3. "The Science Behind Tapping" by Peta Stapleton, Ph.D. - This book dives into the research and scientific evidence behind EFT, exploring how and why it works. A must-read for parents and professionals who want a deeper understanding of tapping.
4. Online Tapping Courses - There are many online courses available that teach EFT for both adults and children. Some reputable options include The Tapping Solution's "Tapping for Kids" course and Brad Yates' "Tapping for Children" program.
5. EFT Practitioner Directory - If you're looking for a qualified EFT practitioner to work with you and your child, check out the practitioner directories on the EFT Universe (www.eftuniverse.com) and EFT International (www.eftinternational.org) websites.

Remember, the more you learn about EFT and how to use it effectively, the better equipped you'll be to support your child's emotional journey. Keep exploring, keep tapping, and enjoy the magic of emotional freedom!

Glossary of Terms

Acupressure Points - Specific points on the body that are stimulated in Traditional Chinese Medicine to balance energy flow. EFT uses a selection of these points in its tapping sequence.

Aspects - Different parts or angles of an emotional issue or memory. In EFT, it's important to tap on all the aspects of a problem for full resolution.

Emotional Freedom Techniques (EFT) - A mind-body technique that combines elements of acupressure, neuro-linguistic programming, and energy psychology to address emotional challenges.

Energy Psychology - A branch of psychology that focuses on the relationship between the mind, body, and energy systems, including meridians and chakras.

Karate Chop Point - The fleshy outer edge of the hand, used as a tapping point in EFT.

Meridians - Energy pathways in the body, as defined by Traditional Chinese Medicine.

Reminder Phrase - A word or short phrase used while tapping to keep the mind focused on the issue being addressed.

Setup Statement - A phrase used at the beginning of an EFT sequence to acknowledge the problem and affirm self-acceptance. Typically follows the format, "Even though I have this [problem], I deeply and completely accept myself."

Tapping - The act of gently stimulating acupressure points on the face and body in an EFT sequence.

9 Gamut Procedure - An addition to the basic EFT sequence that involves tapping on the Gamut point (on the back of the hand) while performing a series of eye movements and other actions. Used to engage different parts of the brain.

This content is provided for informational and educational purposes only and should not be construed as professional advice or a substitute for seeking appropriate professional assistance.

The information presented herein is based on the authors' personal experiences, research, and opinions, which may not be suitable or applicable for all individuals or situations.

The authors, publishers, and distributors have made reasonable efforts to ensure the accuracy and timeliness of the information contained herein. However, they do not guarantee the completeness, suitability, or applicability of this information for any specific individual, situation, or purpose. The authors, publishers, and distributors shall not be held liable for any direct, indirect, incidental, or consequential damages resulting from the use or misuse of the information provided.

It is strongly recommended that readers seek professional advice and guidance from qualified professionals in their respective fields, such as financial advisors, legal counsel, medical practitioners, or certified coaches, for their specific situations and needs.

No part of this content may be reproduced, distributed, or transmitted in any form or by any means, including photocopying, recording, or other electronic or mechanical methods, without the prior written permission of the authors or copyright holders.

For other books and resources that may interest you, please click here:

https://go.howtoalways.win/jacknraven

Made in United States
Orlando, FL
04 March 2025